leadership *called* leadership *is not* leadership

charles hardman

a guidebook for new and not so new leaders

Copyright © Charles Hardman 2025

First Edition

5Ds.com.au

The moral right of the author has been asserted in accordance with the Copyright Amendment (Moral Rights) Act 2000.

All rights reserved. Except as permitted under the Australian Copyright Act 1968 (for example, fair dealing for the purposes of study, research, criticism or review) no part of this publication may be reproduced, stored in a retrieval system, or transmitted in any form or by any means, electronic, mechanical, photocopying, recording or otherwise, without the written permission of the publisher.

No artificial intelligence was used in the creation of this work.

 A catalogue record for this work is available from the National Library of Australia

https://www.nla.gov.au/collections

Title:	Leadership called leadership is not leadership
Author:	Hardman, Charles
ISBN:	978-1-7635713-5-8 (paperback)
	978-1-7635713-6-5 (ebook – epub)
Subjects:	LEADERSHIP / Management / Business / Psychology

Cover design and layout by Charles Hardman

published by inspirationism

To everyone I've worked with ...

Thank you!

1. Introductions

It's an interesting title, but what does it mean?

How can leadership called leadership not be leadership?

I promise I'll get to that in a moment, but first, a few introductions so you can decide whether this book is for you and worth an hour of your time.

i.   **Who am I?**

Hi, my name's Charles! We may have worked together in the past, and/or may work together in the future. I've practiced leadership for about thirty years, and if I'm lucky, I'll practice it for thirty more.

I've worked with small and large organisations, small family run businesses, multinational corporations, not-for-profits (profit-for-purpose), and arts organisations, and I've been employed or contracted in many different roles in a variety of disciplines and industries. From frontline to middle management to senior management, to director and non-executive director.

Since 2010, I've trained, coached, mentored, consulted for, and advised organisations on leadership and management and strategies/tactics for how to achieve their goals.

I have a Master of Professional Education & Training (Workplace Vocation Education and Training); yes, that's its genuine eleven-word title, and a Diploma in Psychology (Organisational), which is actually a Graduate Diploma in Psychology, but I wasn't granted the word 'Graduate' on my diploma because I hadn't completed an undergraduate degree at the time …

I'm a lifelong learner and I enjoy just about everything to do with leadership, psychology, and the nature of learning.

If you're interested in knowing a little bit more about my own leadership journey, there's some more about me at the end of the book.

ii.   What's this book about?

Leadership.

During my career, I've had the privilege of working with thousands of people all over the world, engaging with them and their thoughts on leadership, and how'd they'd describe effective leadership (from their own personal perspective).

Remarkably, the feedback has been consistent across roles, organisations, industries, cultures, countries, and generations, and even though the workplace has changed significantly during these years, the descriptions of the principles and practices for effective leadership have not.

For the first time in history, we have six different generations working side-by-side in the workforce, and even though each generation comes with their own unique wants and needs, the practices required for effective leadership for each generation are the same.

This guidebook condenses thousands of conversations into about nine thousand words to describe the nine principles and nine practices for effective leadership (that's a lot of nines, I know!).

iii.   Why have I written it?

Leadership is my sport.

I spectate leadership the way others spectate football. I 'ooh' and 'ahh' at strategic plays and well-executed skills, and grimace at the own goals and missed opportunities. I analyse the players and the game like a pundit and enjoy comparing actual results with the intended ones.

As mentioned earlier, I have a passion for psychology and education, and leadership is a subset of both. I like knowing how people work, but more than that, I want to know why.

Why do you do the things you do? Why do you believe what you believe, and why do you act and react in the ways you do? Why do I do the things I do? Why do I believe what I believe, and why do I act and react in the ways I do?

Genetics aside, it's because our actions, thoughts, and beliefs are all programmed by others from our earliest age and continue to be programmed by others for all the years of our life. The challenge for us, is to learn the coding, so we can reprogramme ourselves in a way we'd prefer to be.

All of this applies to leadership.

I take the role of leadership very seriously and always have. To impact the lives of others (for better or worse) is one of the greatest responsibilities we have. To be the reason someone has a good day or bad, or why someone enjoys their work or doesn't, is both humbling and daunting.

I've written this book to help others have a more positive impact on those they lead.

iv. How is it going to help?

That's for you and your team members to decide!

You may already do everything this book suggests and need to do no more. Or you may be doing things in your own way and are open to trying something new. You may choose to experiment with these practices, or you may choose to do the opposite. Either way, it's important for you to make your own decisions, and for you to do what you're doing consciously, rather than subconsciously.

Regardless of whether you agree or disagree with the principles and practices outlined in this book, raising them out of the subconscious and into the conscious for open consideration and conversation is how I hope this book will help.

v. Leadership examples

There are an infinite number of situations in which leadership exists, and an infinite number of examples to illustrate effective leadership in these situations. For this reason, and to honour the complexities and intricacies of leadership, this book includes very few examples.

Please apply the principles and practices of leadership to your own situations (hypothetical or real) and your own circumstances to develop your own examples to examine how they fit into your world, and how they would play out for you and your team members.

vi.　Antinomy

If you haven't heard of antinomy before, let me introduce you.

Antinomy is when opposing ideas can be true at the same time. It's when contradictions can coexist in the same place and at the same time and can both be true. It's when, for you to be right, I don't need to be wrong.

An example of an antinomy is in this statement: 'there is no absolute truth'. The statement presents itself as an absolute truth, but at the same time, it denies the absolute truth within it.

If the concept of antinomy boggles your brain, it's important to know from the outset, that leadership is riddled with antinomies, which takes us back to the title of this book, leadership called leadership is not leadership.

vii. Leadership called leadership is not leadership

The title of this book is an adaptation of a verse from Tao Te Ching by Lao-Tzu. In that book, the text reads, 'Tao called Tao, is not Tao'. Simply translated, this means, 'The path called the path, is not the path'.

It's a philosophical principle which implies that when you think you're on the right track, you're not. When you think you know it all, you don't, and when you think you've made it, you haven't. It implies that when you name it, it ceases to exist.

I believe this premise is well suited to leadership, as it encourages us to embark on an endless pursuit of discovery, learning, practice, and of never quite being on the right path. It encourages us to continually strive for better.

Another reason for why leadership called leadership is not leadership, is because leadership has nothing to do with the leader and everything to do with the people being led.

Leadership is a feeling felt by others.

As soon as you think you're a leader, you're not. As soon as you call yourself a leader, you're not. As soon as you think you've mastered leadership, you haven't.

So, what's the purpose of this book again?

Effective leadership lasts for a split-second before it evaporates and is replaced with a new situation, and a new opportunity for effective leadership.

viii.   What's the purpose of a leader?

To lead, but what does that mean?

Is it to provide direction? Instructions and signage can do that.

Is it to keep you on track? A narrow path and short rope can do that.

Is it to inspire and motivate? Posters and memes can do that.

Or is it someone who believes in you and will help you achieve your goals? A partner or parent can fulfill that role (... and can also do the opposite!).

What do leaders bring to the table that does not exist without them?

What are each of us missing in ourselves to make leaders a necessity?

Here's a fun exercise. Imagine a world with no leaders. No leaders in government, not in religion, not in sport, and not in the workplace; imagine there are no leaders anywhere.

What would that world look like?

What would normal people like you and me, need to ensure the world could still function?

What would we need to be self-led?

They're big questions, but your answers will help you answer the question of the purpose of a leader.

As a leader, are you fulfilling the purpose of leadership as defined by you?

ix. What is leadership if it's not leadership?

I've already used the word 'leadership' a lot (235 times in fact), but what does it mean?

There are several definitions of leaders and leadership that you can look up when you're ready, but the simplest one I've ever heard is, 'has followers'. Whilst true enough, this two-word definition doesn't provide any qualitative detail on whether those followers are happy or sad, willing or reluctant, or thriving or surviving.

Other definitions use words like 'charismatic', 'motivational' and 'inspirational' but I'm not sure I fully agree. Sure, they're all great traits, but they're highly subjective and not everyone has the personality to be great at these things. It may also be true that no amount of charisma is able to motivate and inspire the unmotivated and uninspired.

Rather than trying to find the one true definition of leadership, the following pages will describe the principles and practices necessary for effective leadership.

For me, the word leadership has no definition without it being felt by those being led.

x. Styles of leadership

There are many styles of leadership, and much has been written about each one. There's democratic and autocratic, delegative and authoritative, consultative, coercive, transactional, participative, hands-off, bureaucratic, servant, and variations and combinations of each.

There's been enough debate by others, on the pros and cons of each of the styles, so this book won't replicate the same. If you're keen to know more about the styles, please search the internet and/or your local bookshop to find out more.

As a leader, it's important to be able to identify and name your default style of leadership, so you can know what to keep doing and what you need to change.

xi. Leadership traits

Again, enough has been written about the personality traits and attributes of effective leaders, so I won't be delving into too much detail.

Basic human goodness like kindness, care, trust, respect, patience, optimism, open communication, and showing appreciation are all precursors of effective leadership, and if you're missing some or all of these traits, then the following sections may seem like a bit of a challenge.

xii.   Effective leadership

I should have mentioned this earlier, but each time you read the word 'leadership' in this book, please know that I mean 'effective leadership'.

Oxford Languages defines 'effective' as being successful in producing a desired or intended result (languages.oup.com).

Leadership is something you 'do'; however, effective leadership is something others will 'feel'.

If your team member doesn't feel your leadership, it doesn't exist, no matter how hard you're trying. Effective leadership transcends words and actions and focuses on the feelings being felt by those being effectively led.

xiii.   Workplaces

Leadership exists in many environments; within families, sports, religions, schools and universities, government and politics, etc., and whilst the contents of this book may apply to some or all of these environments, its primary focus is on workplaces.

xiv.   Repetition

You may find some repetition in parts of this book as I aim to hammer home several of the points in different ways.

xv. Book structure

If you're happy with what you've read so far, let's get started!

This book is divided into nine sections:

1. Introductions (where we are now)
2. The nine principles of effective leadership
3. The nine practices for effective leadership
4. The three principles of effective management
5. The three practices for effective management
6. A few bonus bits
7. Practices to avoid
8. Summary
9. A little bit more about me

2. The nine principles of effective leadership

The following nine principles provide the foundation for the nine practices in the subsequent section. They are the prerequisites and assumptions on which the next section is based.

If you vehemently disagree with these nine principles, then you'll likely disagree with the nine practices … and that's absolutely okay.

The nine principles of effective leadership

　　i.　Leadership is unlearning
　　ii.　Leadership is not management
　　iii.　Leadership is followership
　　iv.　Leadership must be individualised
　　v.　Leadership has no ego
　　vi.　Leadership ability doesn't come from technical ability
　　vii.　Leadership takes time
　　viii.　Leadership isn't a skill
　　ix.　Leadership is a practice

i. Leadership is unlearning

Our knowledge of leadership is bound by our ability to understand leadership, and we can only ever know leadership as we think it is, and not necessarily as it actually is. (You may need to read that sentence a few times!)

John Singleton's 1995 film, Higher Learning, ends with a single word on the screen. Unlearn.

That word still has a profound effect on me, as it sums up the single and most necessary precursor for all learning:

Unlearning.

Keeping your old principles and practices in place whilst learning new ones is next to impossible. We need to let go of the old, to enjoy the new. We need to unlearn what we know, in order to learn new knowledge. If we're not open to new information, especially information contradictory to what we know, then we'll likely be resistant to it.

Our first learnings of leadership (and management for that matter) came from our parents/guardians, aunts/uncles, grandparents, carers, teachers, sports coaches, media (and social media) personalities, characters on TV and film, and from our first (second, third, etc.) workplace leaders and managers.

Everything we know about leadership and management or think we know about leadership and management has been learnt from others. Our thoughts, beliefs, customs, rituals, and habits about leadership are adopted and amalgamated from those around us.

We copy what we like, and do the opposite of what we don't, but just because a leadership technique works well with one person on one occasion, doesn't mean it will work well with them again, or with others.

Leadership involves continuous unlearning, and if you're not learning by leading, or leading by learning, you're probably doing it wrong. You will learn more from practicing leadership than learning about leadership.

To learn leadership, we need to unlearn leadership.

Leadership is unlearning.

Questions:
- Reflect on a leader you thought was great. What was so great about them?
- Reflect on a manager you despised. What did you loathe about them?
- Where do your beliefs about leadership come from?
- Where do your leadership practices come from?
- How would you like them to be different?

leadership called leadership is not leadership

Notes / Thoughts / Feelings / Reflections

charles hardman

Notes / Thoughts / Feelings / Reflections

ii. Leadership is not management

... and management is not leadership.

If you have people reporting through to you, you have leadership responsibilities and you have management responsibilities, and each set of responsibilities is different from the other.

Leadership is about people, and management is about processes (and everything else).

Leaders DO NOT manage people. They manage the processes that support people.

The primary reason many leaders aren't as effective as they'd like to be, is because they don't know the difference between leadership and management; and therefore, don't know which one they're doing or when.

Leadership zooms out to take the widest possible view, whereas management zooms in to take the narrowest.

Prior to 1980 or 1990, if you were a leader of people, you were called a supervisor, and it was a supervisor's job to supervise a group of others and to tell them how to do their jobs. A supervisor's job description was simple; ensure employees did a good job so they could keep their jobs, or if not, fire those employees and hire and train new ones.

Supervisors reported to managers and managers reported to other managers or to a CEO or a Board. Back then, the employment equation was simple, and leadership (or leadership psychology) was viewed as largely unnecessary, if thought about at all. Back then, bullying was a valid management style and psychological wellbeing was ignored.

People and Culture (or Human Resources) was called Personnel or Payroll, and their tasks were oriented towards those processes.

Between then and now, Supervisors were rebranded Managers or Team Leaders, and the people in these roles were given 'leadership' tasks such as reviewing performance and coaching. These new tasks created new industries devoted to management training, but the vast majority of the management courses miss the point: that management tasks cannot be completed without leadership practices.

Management and leadership are different, even though the people performing them are often the same. Management and leadership require different skillsets and different practices, and each cannot be done effectively, if they're being done concurrently.

Leadership will be ineffective if you try to practice both leadership and management simultaneously.

Leaders who are managers (and managers who are leaders), need to lead people whilst sequentially managing the processes around people. The most important thing to know is, which one are you doing and when.

Leadership should always come first.

Ask yourself: Am I leading (people), or am I managing (processes)? Which one is necessary right now?

Example – Your team member calls in sick for the tenth time this month.

Leadership takes a person-focused view first, asking them if they'd like to share the details of their absence, and asking them, how you (and the organisation) can better support them to perform their role based on their personal situation.

Management takes a process-focused view second, asking the person to lodge their absence into the system with the requisite evidence, and letting them know they have no paid leave left.

In every situation, leadership must come first, and when necessary, management can come second.

People first, processes second.

Leadership is about people, nothing more, nothing less.

Management is about everything else.

Leadership is not management.

Questions:

- How can you better differentiate between leadership and management for yourself?
- How can you separate your practices associated with leadership and management?
- When it comes to people, how can you ensure you put leadership first on every occasion?

Notes / Thoughts / Feelings / Reflections

iii. Leadership Is followership

The original title of this book was going to be, 'If you're leading from the front, you're probably doing it wrong', as the idea of a leader standing at the front of a group telling them what to do, and how to do it, is as antiquated as the pre-1990s' supervisor-driven workplaces.

All leaders are followers, and none of us exist alone at the top of our tree. CEO's have Boards, and Boards have shareholders. Queens and Kings have subjects, and politicians have voters.

Whether we like it or not, we are all led by others, which means we are all experienced followers, and as all leaders have followers, it pays to understand the characteristics which make a follower effective.

The number one characteristic of an effective follower is the ability to listen.

Practicing the qualities of an effective follower will help make you an effective leader.

Leadership is followership.

Questions:

- What are the other attributes of an effective follower?
- How can you develop and use these attributes to be a more effective leader?
- How can you follow the lead of those you are leading to be a more effective leader?

leadership called leadership is not leadership

Notes / Thoughts / Feelings / Reflections

charles hardman

Notes / Thoughts / Feelings / Reflections

iv. Leadership must be individualised

Imagine each of your team members are different zoo animals. Some are small, some are large, some are wild, and others are more domesticated. Some are dangerous and others are playful.

As the leader of the zoo, how will you ensure each has what they need to be safe and comfortable? Do you treat each one in the same way, or will you need to tailor your approach?

Leadership practices that may work with one person may not work with another, and the practices that work on one day may not work on another.

- Different people require individualised leadership practices.
- Different days require individualised leadership practices.
- Different circumstances require individualised leadership practices.

Sorry for the repetition, but it's important to know that for leadership to be effective, leadership practices must be individualised to the person, time, and circumstance.

Leadership is dynamic and forever evolving.

Leadership of a group will only be effective when the leadership of everyone within the group is individualised.

Management on the other hand is different.

- Different people require consistent management practices.
- Different days require consistent management practices.
- Different circumstances require consistent management practices.

Again, sorry for the repetition, but it's important to know that for management to be effective, management must be consistent across people, time, and circumstance.

Management is relatively static; the practices must remain the same (more on this later).

Leadership must be individualised.

Questions:

- How do you feel about individualising your leadership practices for each of your team members?
- How much extra time do you think it will take?
- What resources and support will you need to individualise your leadership practices?

leadership called leadership is not leadership

Notes / Thoughts / Feelings / Reflections

charles hardman

Notes / Thoughts / Feelings / Reflections

v. Leadership has no ego

On my first day studying counselling, the lecturer stood at the front of the theatre and announced, "The ultimate aim of counselling is for your client to call you up after a number of sessions to tell you, 'I'm not coming in to see you anymore and I'm not sure why I started seeing you in the first place'."

What she was saying, was that the ultimate aim of counselling was for your client to believe they were always the way they are now (after your help) and hasn't ever needed your help to get them there. What she was saying, was that being made redundant was the true sign of success.

How does the idea of actively working towards your own redundancy feel to you?

It knocked the wind out of me when I first heard it and there's still an echo of that feeling now. Regardless, she was one hundred percent right. Counselling is not about the counsellor; it is wholly about the client. The counsellor's ego should play no part in the relationship. Likewise, leadership should never be about the leader, it should only be about the team member.

Imagine, after working tirelessly with a team member to develop them, could your ego handle being told by them that you have no purpose, and that you possibly never had any purpose? Could you accept their statements as indicators of a job well done, or would you need to explain yourself, thus undoing all your good work?

Is the ultimate goal of leadership to lead your team members to be self-led?

Is the ultimate goal of all leaders to make themselves unnecessary?

Your answers to these questions will lead you towards (or away) from these aims. If you agree, your subconscious will work towards it, and if you disagree, then your subconscious will work against it.

Effective leadership is altruistic and aims to make leadership redundant.

Leadership has no ego.

Questions:

- How does your ego guide your leadership behaviours?
- How comfortable are you with the notion of actively working towards your own redundancy?
- In your leadership practices, how do your behaviours insulate or protect your ego?

leadership called leadership is not leadership

Notes / Thoughts / Feelings / Reflections

charles hardman

Notes / Thoughts / Feelings / Reflections

vi. Leadership ability doesn't come from technical ability

The biggest mistake made by leaders and managers in every organisation around the world, is promoting people who are good at their jobs into leadership roles, with the assumption they'll be good at that too.

I saw it all the time in the contact centre industry. The best call makers/takers would be promoted to be team leaders of other call makers/takers, and everyone around me would scratch their heads wondering why service levels dropped soon after.

Being good at a job doesn't automatically make a person good at making other people good at their jobs.

Technical expertise in a job does not equal technical expertise in leadership. People who are effective at their jobs will not automatically be effective at leading other people to be effective at their jobs.

In sports, a great player doesn't automatically make a great coach, and sometimes, a great coach is someone who has never played the game.

It's the same with leadership.

Leaders should be hired based on their ability to lead.

Leadership ability doesn't come from technical ability.

Questions:

- Does your organisation promote people into leadership roles based on how good they are at their jobs?
- Is it fair to promote people who are good at their jobs into positions of leadership? (If yes, fair to whom?)
- How can people who are good at their jobs be supported to be effective leaders?

leadership called leadership is not leadership

Notes / Thoughts / Feelings / Reflections

charles hardman

Notes / Thoughts / Feelings / Reflections

vii. Leadership takes time

The secret ingredient to effective leadership is time.

Effective leadership takes time to do well.

Effective leaders have time for their team members and prioritise their time towards them.

Effective leadership is not efficient.

- Efficiency is about doing as much as you can, in the shortest possible time.
- Effectiveness is about doing something properly for the best possible outcome.

There is no such thing as efficient leadership.

Efficiency is the antithesis of effectiveness.

Imagine you have fifteen team members and are about to introduce some new technology which will affect each of them in different ways.

The efficient way to communicate the changes, would be to send an email or message to all fifteen, but that will mean you'll need to communicate all the changes to the entire group, whether they effect the individuals or not.

The effective way would be to hold fifteen individual meetings so you can tailor the communication to each person's needs, and engage them in what they need to know.

Emails (and messaging applications) are the enemy of effective leadership.

Leadership takes time. A lot of time.

Questions:

- How much time do you prioritise to leadership tasks compared to management tasks?
- How do you try to be efficient in your leadership tasks?
- How do you try to be effective in your leadership tasks?

leadership called leadership is not leadership

Notes / Thoughts / Feelings / Reflections

viii. Leadership isn't a skill

Leadership is a group of practices.

Effective leadership includes training, facilitation, coaching, mentoring, consulting, advising, and communicating.

Could you be an effective leader without performing any of these tasks?

How successful would you be?

Effective leaders don't focus on being effective leaders, they focus on being effective at all the other activities to make them effective leaders.

On its own, leadership isn't a skill.

Questions:

- How effective are you at training, facilitation, coaching, mentoring, consulting, advising, and communicating?
- How do you measure how effective you are at these activities?
- What resources and support do you need to be more effective at these activities?

leadership called leadership is not leadership

Notes / Thoughts / Feelings / Reflections

ix. Leadership is a practice

Within meditation practices, it is often said that the aim of meditation isn't to become good at meditation, it's to become good at practicing meditation. The aim isn't to become a great meditator, it's to become diligent in your practice of meditation.

The same applies to leadership.

Your aim shouldn't be great leadership; your aim should be great leadership practices.

Your aim shouldn't be to become an effective leader; your aim should be to practice effective leadership.

Effective leadership is a series of practices that are only effective when you're doing them. Learnings from practicing feed into new practices and newer learnings feed into newer practices. The cycle is continuous without end.

In leadership, practice does not make perfect. The aim of the leadership practices is to practice leadership. Practice takes leadership, but also builds leadership.

When you stop practicing, leadership stops with it.

Leadership is a verb, not a noun.

Leadership is a practice.

The next section describes the nine practices for effective leadership.

3. The nine practices for effective leadership

The following nine practices are built on the foundation of the nine principles in the previous section. They are the practical things you can do right now to practice effective leadership.

It's important to note that these practices may seem to have no immediate impact, and if you thrive on instant gratification, then these practices may be a challenge for you.

Each of the nine practices is a long-term proposition with long-term results. Each will cultivate effective leadership whilst your leadership relationship exists.

The nine practices are not presented in a priority order and are not sequential.

They are only effective when you're practicing them, and effective leaders practice all nine all of the time.

The nine practices for effective leadership

 i. Ask questions
 ii. Get to know your people
 iii. Empathy and compassion
 iv. Self-regulation
 v. Integrity
 vi. Tell the story
 vii. Engage
 viii. Steer
 ix. Boundaries

i. Ask questions

Effective leaders ask questions and listen to the answers with an open mind. They are happy to play in the space between knowing and questioning, between practice and curiosity, and in the practice of curiosity.

Effective leaders remain perpetually curious and are always asking questions; not to be annoying, but to find out why things are being done the way they are. Whilst they're interested in the whats, hows, whos, and whens, it's the whys they're most keen to understand. Understanding the whys help effective leaders understand behaviour, and understanding behaviour is key to effective leadership.

Asking questions seems simple enough, but for the practice to be effective, leaders require three things –

1. suspension of their bias and judgment,
2. an open mind, and
3. verbal and non-verbal communication to demonstrate the above.

Suspending bias and judgment is easier said than done, however, genuine curiosity helps. I avoided titling this practice, 'Be curious', as there is a much-shared scene of the TV show, Ted Lasso, where protagonist Ted delivers a monologue on 'being curious' whilst playing darts with antagonist Rupert. I won't spoil the scene for anyone who hasn't seen it, but it's a great little reminder that curiosity can easily override bias and judgement (if we let it).

Keeping an open mind is also easier said than done, but it's a skill worth developing if you want to practice effective leadership. The first step to an open mind is neutrality, and the second step is equanimity.

Equanimity has many definitions, but the simplest one is to 'be unaffected'. It's a type of unattachment to your thoughts, beliefs, and behaviours, and those of others. It's an easy-goingness, a calmness and composure, and a mental balance and even mindedness. Equanimity allows an openness to hear what is being said without latching on to it or pushing it away; it allows the answers to be as they are. Equanimity also helps with suspending bias and judgement.

Effective leaders also encourage others to ask questions, suspend their judgement, and to keep an open mind.

Effective leaders feed their team members' curiosity by taking the time to explain the whys, as much as they would explain the whats, hows, whos, and whens. We've all been in situations where we've been told what to do, without being told why, and we all know how that feels.

Asking questions, and being asked questions, opens your personal perception into a broader perspective.

Effective leaders ask questions and encourage others to ask questions of them.

Practical tips:

- To be neutral, let things be as they are, rather than the way you think they are.
- Before asking questions (about why), think of at least three different possible answers. *
- Before asking questions (about why), think of what could be said to make you critical, defensive, or want to retaliate. *

*   Time travel is real. Simply close your eyes and imagine different versions of the future, based on making different choices right now.

charles hardman

Notes / Thoughts / Feelings / Reflections

ii. Get to know your people

Knowing your people is a prerequisite for effective leadership, because if you don't know them, how can you know how to lead them?

Many leaders get to know their people on a personal level with the aim of building rapport and personal relationships. They aim to maximise their similarities and minimise their differences to create friendships and a harmonious working environment. This works well until it doesn't, and you're forced to pull rank to get something done. Personal relationships don't necessarily help with professional relationships, and in many cases, they can act as a hinderance.

Effective leadership is based on professional relationships.

Effective leaders get to know their people on a professional level and let their people get to know them in the same way. Most workplaces are professional environments, so it makes sense to get to know your team members professionally -

- What are their career aspirations?
- What are they trying to achieve in their job, or in their professional life?
- Why are they in the job they're in?
- What inspires them at work?
- What motivates them at work?
- How can you, as a leader, fit into all of this?
- How do they want to be led?
- What do they need from you?
- How can you support them?
- How can you help them achieve what they want to?

Many people will never have been asked these questions, so don't be surprised if some don't have answers. Give them time and space and revisit the questions regularly to ensure your understanding remains valid over time.

Effective leaders know the answers to these questions for themselves and will share them with their team members. Much has been said about authenticity and vulnerability in leadership (not in this book though!) and this can be a great way to start.

If you or your team members can't answer these questions, find resources to help. There are many personality questionnaires and type indicators on the market, but my personal favourite is 16Personalities (16personalities.com). They offer a free personality assessment that uses a five-factor model to help people understand how they perceive the world and how they can optimally operate within different environments (e.g. friendships, relationships, workplaces, etc.). *

Getting to know your people will help you discover which leadership style they need from you. Whilst there may be pros and cons of each of the leadership styles mentioned earlier (democratic, autocratic, delegative, authoritative, consultative, coercive, transactional, participative, hands-off, bureaucratic, servant, etc.), knowing what your team members need from you and how they want to be led will help you know which style you'll need to adopt for each of them (whether you like the style or not).

Effective leaders know their people professionally, and allow their people to know them in the same way.

Practical tips:

- Ask more questions of a professional nature.
- If you use a personality questionnaire or type indicator, use them as team building exercises so team members can get to know each other as well.
- Never, ever use someone's personality type or type indicator as a label for them. They exist to learn preferences only!

* I have no relationship, professional or otherwise with 16Personalities or NERIS Analytics Limited. I simply like their work!

iii. Empathy and compassion

I find empathy a fascinating concept as it's more than sympathy and more than walking in someone else's shoes.

Empathy is a felt feeling, and if someone needs to physically experience the experience of another to feel empathy, then that's not empathy. Empathy is being able to feel, understand, and appreciate another's feelings and experiences without needing to physically experience those feelings or experiences.

Rather than having empathy or not having empathy, we all exist at different points along an empathy spectrum. Imagine a linear scale of 0 to 10, where someone who is 0 has no empathy for anyone but themselves (someone with psychopathy/sociopathy/narcissism), and 10 is someone who has unbridled empathy for others (someone with clairempathy/clairsentience).

- Do you think having too much empathy is as problematic as having too little?
- Where do you think effective leadership should be on the empathy spectrum?
- Where are you on the empathy spectrum? If you don't know, there are online questionnaires to find out.
- Do you think it's possible for a person to shift their position higher or lower?
- If it is, how would they go about it?

I'll leave you to ponder these philosophical questions, but my answer to the question about effective leadership is 6 or 7, to ensure their empathy is balanced. Too little, and they'll care about nothing except themselves, and too much, they'll be conflicted and debilitated by caring too much about everyone else's circumstances.

If empathy is described as an inner feeling, then compassion needs to be its outward expression. On its own, empathy has little use; it's what's done with it that matters.

Effective leaders need to have empathy and compassion for each of their team members, but also for themselves, their manager, employer, customers, shareholders, etc.

Effective leaders also foster an environment for their team members to have empathy and compassion for each other, for themselves, for you, and for everyone else.

A healthy level of empathy and compassion is a prerequisite for effective leadership.

Leaders who have a lower level of empathy can still show compassion. They can still ask more questions.

Effective leaders practice empathy and encourage empathy in their team members. They use their empathy to show compassion.

Practical tips:
- If you feel you have low empathy, ask more questions to increase your understanding of someone else's feelings and experiences.
- If you feel you have high empathy, learn to set yourself boundaries. More on this later.
- Discuss empathy and compassion with your team to help define a realistic and common understanding for your workplace.

iv. Self-regulation

At some point in your life, you will have heard the term 'emotional intelligence', and if you haven't as yet, then the time is now!

Emotional intelligence is the ability to understand, manage, and use emotions effectively. It's more than self-awareness, and more than empathy; it's about how you use both to regulate your own behaviour and reactions.

Effective leaders are aware of their own attitudes and behaviours, preferences and biases, and likes and dislikes; and are aware that these are not necessarily shared by others. They are also aware of how their attitudes and behaviours, preferences and biases, and likes and dislikes affect others, and know how those of others, affect them.

Effective leaders regulate their communication, verbal and non-verbal: what they say, and how they say it (words, tone, volume, speed, expressions, gestures, and body language).

Effective leaders self-regulate by –

- taking time to pause,
- practicing patience and equanimity,
- identifying their emotions via self-reflection,
- managing their emotions in a productive way, and
- understanding what irritates them and knowing how to calm themselves before reacting.

Effective leaders understand that honesty, authenticity, and vulnerability in leadership still need to be regulated, and that their triggers are their own to manage, not someone else's responsibility to tread lightly around them.

Effective leaders understand that honesty, authenticity, and vulnerability in their team members also need to be regulated, and that their team members' triggers are their own to manage, not others to own (within reason!).

When talking about self-regulation, it's beneficial to know what dysregulation looks like, so you can know what you shouldn't be doing. John Gottman (gottman.com) describes four dysregulated behaviours which severely impact all relationships (these will impact your personal relationships too!). They are –

- criticism,
- defensiveness,
- contempt, and
- stonewalling.

Effective leaders do not engage in these behaviours.

Effective leaders want to know 'why?'. They know how to pause between an action and reaction, between a request, and their response. They give themselves time and space to think about events, or to adequately consider requests before responding. They know that urgency (real or contrived) can lead to dysregulation.

Effective leaders practice self-regulation and create environments which encourage their team members to self-regulate.

Practical tips:

- Time travel. Pause and take time before you react or respond.
- Always be kind and respectful.
- Ask for feedback on how you handle situations.

v. Integrity

Leaders lead by example, but integrity is so much more than that.

Integrity is doing the right thing even when no one is looking; it's honour, honesty, respect, and truthfulness; for yourself, for others, and for the rules.

To be an effective leader, integrity is vital in what you say, what you do, how you behave, and how you talk about others.

There's a famous (or infamous) line in an interview between journalist David Frost and President Richard Nixon about his abuses of power. When asked about them, President Nixon replies along the lines of, *when the president does it, it means it's not illegal.* It was a watershed moment related to the Watergate scandal.

I'm reminded of this response each time I see a manager doing something they shouldn't, especially when they're doing it out in the open. It's as though they believe their title entitles them to do as they please without consequence, however there are always consequences.

If managers hold themselves to a lesser standard than what they would expect from their team members, they need to adequately explain why. Is it because they own the business and have earned the perks? Or is it because they are paid more? Or because they deserve some leeway because they have extra responsibilities and work longer hours? For what it's worth, I don't believe any of these explanations are adequate, but I'm not the one who needs to be convinced.

Practicing integrity is the easiest of the nine practices outlined in this book because it requires no special skills or knowledge to perform well.

Effective leaders have unwavering integrity and expect integrity from their team members.

Practical tips:

- Abide by the same rules as your team members or renegotiate the rules for everyone.
- Never, ever do something you'd reprimand your team member for doing.
- Never, ever talk about your team members behind their backs (no matter how private you think the conversations are).

vi. Tell the story

Effective leaders know how to tell a good story.

This practice was originally called communication, as all components of communication are vital for leadership; however, effective storytelling is essential for effective leadership.

Verbal storytelling is the oldest form of communication between humans, and everyone loves a good story! Stories help us engage with all that has happened before and help take us on a journey to where we are going. Stories are critical for empathy.

In the workplace, leaders are given access to see more of the moving parts in a system and can see the connections between people, tasks, the work, and the goals. They can see cause and effect.

Because of this, they see the bigger picture of what's going on, and how everyone fits into that picture. Effective leaders use the bigger picture to tell a bigger story, so team members know where, when, how, and why they fit in.

Effective leaders use their organisation's vision, mission, and values to tie their team members to the bigger organisational story.

Storytelling takes more time than barking out orders, and effective leaders take the time to tell the story; from the beginning, through the middle, to the end; to where we are now, and where we want to be.

Effective leaders tell good stories and are also interested in the stories of others.

Practical tips:

- Ask team members how much of the story they want or need to hear.
- Ask your team members how they want the story told.
- When you don't know the story, ask for it. Don't make stories up!

vii. Engage

Effective leaders continuously engage their team members.

Employee engagement has spawned an entire industry, but at its heart, it's nothing more than the level of active participation an employee has in their job and in their organisation. If they're able to actively participate, then they'll be engaged (and possibly committed and enthusiastic), but if they're not, then you'll get the opposite.

Organisations spend huge amounts of money on fancy reward and recognition and incentive programmes, and on team building, and social events, but many of them haven't yet covered the basics of asking employees what they need/want to do their jobs well.

The simplest thing a leader can do to maintain engagement is to verbalise their appreciation for a job well done.

Team members' engagement will remain in place or will diminish depending on how they are treated.

Most employees are paid for their engagement, so it's important to know what they are being paid for, as well as what they think they are being paid for. Is it for their time, their attendance, their activity, or for outcomes and results, or is it a combination of all of them? Knowing, will help you (and them) know what to focus on.

Effective leaders know what engagement looks like for each of their team members and know how each would like to engage and be engaged in their work, within the team, and within the organisation.

Practical tips:

- Employee engagement is best done face to face.
- Ditch the employee engagement surveys as they are the lowest form of employee engagement, especially when employees are forced to answer questionnaires they haven't been engaged in designing.
- Not every employee wants to be engaged any more than the bare minimum, and there's nothing wrong with that. You can't hold someone accountable to a standard they didn't agree to.

viii. Steer

Leaders keep their hand on the tiller! *

Effective leaders keep one eye on each of their team members, and the other on the bigger picture of the team. Why does the team exist? Why are they in the jobs they're in, and why are you in the job you're in? What are you meant to be doing and what are you meant to be achieving, and to what standard?

Effective leaders use the bigger picture to engage with their team members to develop a team-based vision, mission, and values, as well as team-based goals, objectives, strategies, plans, and actions. They then develop these into specific, measurable, and realistic targets so each team member knows exactly what they are responsible for.

Effective leaders break down the bigger picture into its smaller parts. They steer their team members to stay true to their goals.

Effective leaders gently steer their team members (and the team) in the direction they should be heading in.

---

*   A tiller is a lever used to steer a boat. 'Hand on the tiller' is an old saying. It means to steer or guide a situation.

Practical tips:

- Know where you're going so it's easier for someone to follow you.
- Use the previous seven practices to help design your goals.
- Take every opportunity, no matter how minor, to steer your team members to stay on track.

ix. Boundaries

The previous eight practices have focussed on your team members and on being the most effective leader for them; however, this ninth practice focuses on you and how you can be the most effective leader for yourself.

Leadership is situational and circumstantial, and has a line that shouldn't be crossed, and you're the only one who can draw that line.

Leaders who reach an impasse with a team member after practicing all eight of the preceding leadership practices know when to draw that line. They know whether it is them, or their team member who is causing the issue, and they will take appropriate steps to change themselves, and/or request change from their team member, and/or transfer the team member to new leadership, and/or formally manage the performance of the team member (up or out).

Leaders who have tried everything they can to individualise their leadership practices to no avail know their limits.

As mentioned earlier, effective leaders are trainers, facilitators, coaches, mentors, consultants, professional advisors, and expert communicators, but are they therapists? How about umpires? Or judges, or lawyers having to continually argue their case?

If you have the skillsets to do some or all of these things, and are happy to do them, then go for it, but know where you draw the line, and know where your boundaries are. Knowing what you are as a leader, as well as what you are not, is extremely important.

I once had a team member who needed several weeks off due to losing a parent. It was a heartbreaking situation, and I practiced all the practices in this book, but it wasn't enough for her. During her first couple of weeks back, she became more and more agitated with me because I hadn't asked her enough personal questions about her experience of loss.

It wasn't because I wasn't interested, or didn't care, it was because I didn't want to delve into her personal life in that way. I didn't want to cross the line into becoming her psychological counsellor (even though I had the skills and qualifications to do so).

I'd provided her with access to our employee assistance programme (professional counselling) and didn't want to interfere with that. I apologised to her and explained my position, but it didn't change her view (and I didn't need to change it for her, because that too would have been crossing another one of my boundaries).

Leaders know their boundaries, and effective leaders know how to keep them.

Practical tips:

- As a leader, what roles are you happy to take on?
- What roles aren't you happy to take on?
- Design a short leadership charter between you and each of your team members so you know what you can expect from each other. Include contingencies for when expectations aren't being met.

Summary of the principles and practices

So, there you have it! The nine principles and nine practices of effective leaders, as described by thousands of employees during the past thirty-years.

Here's a quick recap -

Summary of the principles of effective leadership

i. To learn leadership, we need to unlearn leadership.
ii. Leadership is about people, nothing more, nothing less. Management is about everything else.
iii. To understand effective leadership, we need to understand effective followership.
iv. Leadership of a group will only work when the leadership of everyone in the group has been individualised.
v. Effective leadership is altruistic and aims to make leadership redundant.
vi. Leaders should be hired based on their ability to lead.
vii. Leadership takes time. It is not efficient.
viii. Effective leaders don't focus on being effective leaders, they focus on being effective at all the other activities to make them effective leaders.
ix. Leadership is a verb, not a noun.

Summary of the practices of effective leaders

i. Asks questions and encourages others to ask questions of them.
ii. Knows their people on a professional level, and encourages their people to know them in the same way.
iii. Practices empathy and compassion, and encourages empathy and compassion in their team members.
iv. Practices self-regulation and creates environments which encourage their team members to self-regulate.
v. Practices unwavering integrity and expects integrity from their team members.
vi. Tells the story and are also interested in the stories of others.
vii. Knows what engagement looks like for each of their team members and knows how'd they'd like to engage and be engaged in their work, within the team, and within the organisation.
viii. Gently steers their team members to stay true to their goals.
ix. Keeps their boundaries.

Effective leadership is practicing all nine, all of the time, and a leader who ceases to practice, ceases to be an effective leader.

Questions:

- Which ones are you already doing, and which ones will you start?
- Do you think you can do all nine at the same time, all of the time?
- And how about management? How does that fit in with all of this?

Well, I'm glad you asked ...

Management called management is management

Management becomes one hundred percent easier when you're practicing effective leadership.

Practicing effective leadership builds trust and respect, and simplifies the principles and practices for effective management.

Practicing effective management also builds trust and respect, and helps set the scene for the principles and practices for effective leadership.

There are three principles of effective management, and three practices for effective management.

I'll keep these short!

4. The three principles of effective management

The following three principles provide the foundation for the three practices in the next section. They are the prerequisites and assumptions on which the next section is based.

They are -

   i. Focus on processes (especially those that relate to people)
   ii. Be consistent
   iii. Be fair

i. **Focus on processes (especially those that relate to people)**

As mentioned in the second principle of effective leadership, leadership is about people, and management is about processes.

Effective management focuses on managing processes, rather than managing people.

To manage processes, you need to have them documented and communicated. Processes include policies and procedures, and these should be referenced in your employment contracts.

In smaller organisations, processes are usually written reactively, however, they should be written proactively so that all new employees know what to expect when they start. Documented processes help resolve issues and challenges as they arise.

Processes should find the middle ground between being overly prescriptive (unless absolutely necessary), and overly open to interpretation. In some cases, processes will be a single paragraph, and in others, a few pages.

At a minimum, ensure your organisation has basic HR processes for behaviour, performance, attendance (and leave), and adherence. In Australia, Fair Work Australia has a number of free templates (fairwork.gov.au).

Effective managers ensure their team members have agreed to these processes.

Effective managers focus on processes.

Questions:

- Which processes do you have documented?
- Which processes do you need documented?
- How are you going to fill in the blanks?

ii. Be consistent

Effective leadership is all about individualisation, whereas effective management is all about being consistent across individuals, time, and circumstance.

Oxford Languages defines 'consistent' as acting in the same way over time, especially so as to be fair (languages.oup.com).

If you can't be consistent across all the team members in your team, you need to have a valid reason (that is understood and respected by your other team members) as to why.

Effective managers are always consistent.

Questions –

- What does consistency mean to you?
- In what situations might you be prevented from being consistent?
- How will you deal with these situations to ensure that others know why you seem to be acting inconsistently?

iii. Be fair

Effective leadership and effective management require you to be fair.

Oxford Languages defines being 'fair' as being impartial and just, without favouritism or discrimination (languages.oup.com).

If you can't be fair to all the team members in your team, you need to have a reason (that is understood and respected by your other team members) as to why.

Effective managers are always fair.

Questions –

- What does fairness mean to you?
- In what situations might you be prevented from being fair?
- How will you deal with these situations to ensure that others know why you seem to be acting unfairly?

5. The three practices for effective management

The following three practices are built on the foundation of the three principles in the previous section. They are the practical things you can do right now to practice effective management.

These practices will have an immediate impact, and if you thrive on instant gratification, then these practices are for you.

The three practices for effective management

i. Involve your team members in designing processes
ii. Involve your team members in designing management scaffolding
iii. Manage behaviour, performance, attendance, and adherence (performance management processes)

i. Involve your team members in designing processes

Whilst this section is about effective management, involving your team members in designing and reviewing your processes will show great leadership, especially around engagement.

Effective managers know that they can't hold someone accountable to processes they don't understand or haven't signed up for.

If you've involved your team members in designing processes, then their understanding and agreement is almost guaranteed.

Practical tips:

- Depending on how many processes you need written, assign one to each of your team members to draft. Have them present their work and take feedback.
- Ensure your processes are referenced in your employment contracts.
- Review processes annually, and ensure they are agreed to.

ii. **Involve your team members in designing management scaffolding**

Management scaffolding is everything else you need to build around your team members to support them and their work.

Involving your team members in designing and reviewing the scaffolding will show great leadership, especially around engagement.

Management scaffolding includes -

1. Organisational values, vision, and mission
2. Code of conduct and behavioural expectations
3. Position descriptions and position purposes
4. Key result areas, and key performance indicators
5. Grievance processes and procedures
6. Recruitment resources
7. Induction training programmes
8. Ongoing professional development programmes
9. Career planning and succession planning

Practical tips:

- Ask your team members to proactively review the scaffolding that already exists, and ask for their help to fill in the blanks.
- Ensure your scaffolding is referenced in your employment contracts.
- Review your scaffolding annually, and ensure it is agreed to.

iii. Manage behaviour, performance, attendance, and adherence (performance management processes)

Effective managers manage processes around behaviour, performance, attendance, and adherence in real time.

Due to your effective leadership practices, you have already asked your team members how they would like to receive feedback (both good and bad, and positive and negative), and have an agreement in place on how to best have the following conversations.

When a team member exceeds your expectations, take them aside and say something immediately. Examples -

- Performs exemplary work
- Goes above and beyond expectations
- Models all the behaviours you expect from them
- Takes on coaching and training roles without being asked

When a team member doesn't meet your expectations, take them aside and say something immediately. Examples -

- Behaves inappropriately
- Performance isn't up to standard
- Attendance isn't up to standard
- Adherence isn't up to standard

Too many managers are in the habit of waiting for negative patterns to emerge before saying something to their team members, not realising that they are actively encouraging the negative patterns to emerge by not saying anything in the first place! (Please read that again!)

Is it because leaders/managers are afraid of managing performance, or is it because they don't have the documented processes to follow? Or is it because they just wished their team members would do the right thing without needing to be told time and again?

Regardless of the reason, poor managers fail to manage behaviour, performance, and attendance in a timely manner, and their failure will affect all others in their team.

The quickest way to turn a high-performing team member into a low-performing team member is to let another team member get away with poor performance.

Workplace culture is 'the way things are done around here'. It is the thoughts, beliefs, customs, rituals, and habits of a group. Many managers fail to see their role in workplace culture, not realising that they 'are' workplace culture.

Managing processes around behaviour, performance, attendance, and adherence in real time isn't scary if you have a process to follow, and the process has been agreed to.

Fair Work Australia (fairwork.gov.au) has some great resources to help. These include –

- A best practice guide to managing performance and underperformance.
- Guides and templates for managing performance and issuing warnings.
- A free online course on how to best manage performance.

Effective managers manage processes around behaviour, performance, attendance, and adherence in real time, and proactively manage these processes by formally checking in with each of their team members at least once per month in a formal/professional setting.

Practical tips:

- Ask questions, listen to the answers, and provide feedback, factually and without judgement or emotion.
- Be kind and respectful, and follow the processes step by step.
- Try not to say things to undermine yourself or the organisation.

charles hardman

Notes / Thoughts / Feelings / Reflections

6. A few bonus bits

i. Where does change management fit in?

Change management (or the need to manage change) is a bit of a misnomer, as change (from a people perspective) shouldn't need to be managed.

If leadership across an entire organisation is effective, change is expected and promoted, and is viewed as constant, and all change management activities can be process-focused.

Effective leaders ensure there are 'no surprises' and are open and honest with their team members (within legal frameworks).

Some managers deliberately withhold information from their team members because they are afraid of the consequences; that they'll see a drop in performance or mass resignations.

Fear leads to poor leadership, and no amount of 'change management' will help fix that.

ii. How about decision making?

It's true ... leaders and managers need to be great at making decisions, however, it's how they go about making those decisions, which will make them effective or not.

Effective decision making comes from the nine practices for effective leadership, and the three principles for effective management. Effective leaders own their decisions.

iii. How about effective communication?

I couldn't finish this book without adding a short section dedicated to communication.

Effective leaders and managers are effective communicators, and effective communicators are usually effective leaders and managers.

Effective communication has many components, but it's only possible when the sender is articulate, the receiver is primed, and when the most appropriate type of communication is used.

Far too often, people communicate in a way that makes their own life easy. Spraying out an email to one-hundred people is easier than calling or meeting one-hundred people, but like effective leadership, effective communication is rarely efficient.

Likewise, people prefer to receive communication in ways which allow them to filter content and assign importance, when neither should be their responsibility. A preference to receive hundreds of text-based messages a day instead of face-to-face communication makes it easier to miss urgent and important information.

Email/Messaging has become the subconscious default communication channel, but should it be?

Make a conscious decision about the best way to communicate before communicating.

Regardless of preference, the hierarchy of effective communication types, from best to worst is –

1. Face to face one-on-one
2. Face to face in a group
3. Video conference one-on-one
4. Video conference in a group
5. Phone call
6. Email
7. Messaging applications
8. Text messaging
9. Posting information on an intranet

That being said, no matter how many ways a message is communicated, or how many times it is communicated, it will be ineffective if the receiver is not primed and not ready to receive it.

A colleague and friend of mine (Hi Graham!) used to continually joke with each other, that our communication was useless until the receiver wanted to know the information.

We could brief someone ten times on something, and they'd still come to see us a week later to ask what was going on.

If the information wasn't important to them at the time we gave it to them, then it wasn't important, no matter how important it was to us. We soon learnt to tell a story which made the information important to them, and which made them want to ask for it earlier.

Effective leaders communicate effectively by knowing when to communicate, and how to communicate.

Effective communication takes time.

charles hardman

Notes / Thoughts / Feelings / Reflections

7. Practices to avoid

This book has covered some ground on all the things you need to do to be an effective leader and manager, but how about the practices you should avoid?

Well, that's easy ...

Here are the nine leadership killers -

   i. Lying
   ii. Not being present, not listening
   iii. Pretending to know
   iv. Being dismissive
   v. Being pessimistic
   vi. Being hypocritical
   vii. Criticism, defensiveness, contempt, and stonewalling
   viii. Reprimanding team members in front of others
   ix. Pulling rank, or refusing to do something you'd ask a team member to do (because you think it's beneath you)

Anyone who engages in any one of the above nine behaviours, loses their credibility, and loses their ability to effectively lead and/or manage.

No ifs, buts, or maybes.

charles hardman

Notes / Thoughts / Feelings / Reflections

8. Summary

Effective leadership is about people, and effective management is about processes (and everything else).

Many leaders lead others in the way they want to be led, not realising that they are not representative of each of their team members.

Treating others the way you want to be treated, doesn't apply in leadership. You need to ask your team members how they want to be treated, and act accordingly.

All humans strive for some semblance of autonomy, independence, and sovereignty, and leaders can stand in the way, when their job is to encourage us forward.

The nine practices of effective leaders are the same nine practices of effective humans.

Leadership is one of the most human things we can do.

To practice being a good leader, we simply need to practice being a good human.

None of this is easy, yet all of it is.

I had to finish this book with an antinomy!

charles hardman

Notes / Thoughts / Feelings / Reflections

9. A little bit more about me

I wanted to get into the workforce as soon as I was able, because I wanted to get out of it just as fast.

During primary school, I wanted to be a car designer. At high school, I wanted to be an artist. By the time I graduated, all I wanted to do was earn money, save money, invest money, and retire early to live off the money. I'd invented the acronym FIRE (financially independent, retire early) without knowing it.

Leadership wasn't an aspiration for me.

My first jobs were burger flipper, retail sales assistant, football umpire, and cloakroom attendant at a nightclub, and I worked all four concurrently whilst at high school.

The jobs gave me exposure to leadership, good, bad, and otherwise, and also gave me my first opportunities to lead others, but it still wasn't something I aspired to do.

During my first year at university, I kept working full-time hours and worked second and third jobs during weeknights and on weekends. Working seven days a week wasn't conducive to studying, and I failed all four of the subjects I was(n't) studying. I was called up by the university's board and threatened with expulsion.

I convinced them to let me stay and took a six-month leave of absence, and at the same time, I started working as a commission-only mobile phone salesperson.

It was during my first few days of induction training, that I discovered what I wanted to do with my life. I wanted to be a workplace trainer.

My sales trainer was easy going, knowledgeable, and treated us with respect and as equals. He was a leader without trying to be one, and someone I wanted to follow.

When I returned to university, I switched my degree to psychology and started learning about learning and the human mind's effect on behaviour. I also started applying for every entry level trainer job that was advertised.

After a year or two, I'd applied for three hundred roles and had been rejected by all three hundred, with each of their response letters being a copy of the previous, 'we require experience'.

I continued to sell mobile phones and completed a certificate in assessment and workplace training on the side, to help bolster my credentials.

I persisted with my search and was eventually offered a contract as a sessional trainer at a college specialising in retail and hospitality. It was for twelve weeks, and the job was to train Certificate II in Retail to a group of long-term unemployed people in regional Victoria.

The role was to train people who didn't want to be there, in something they weren't interested in, just so they could keep receiving their unemployment benefits.

The twelve trainees were in their thirties, forties, and fifties, and I was barely twenty-two with no experience in what I was doing, or what it was like to be in their shoes.

For six hours a day, five days a week, it was my job to lead a group of misfits to be competent in retail with the aim they'd get jobs afterwards. My task wasn't just to teach skills, it was to change their thoughts, attitudes, and behaviours.

I spent the first two weeks 'off script', ignoring the course content, instead, learning about them, their situations, and about their wants and needs, not just from the course, but in life.

By the third week, I'd tailored the modules to what they'd each shared with me, and by the fourth, they could all see the point of what we were doing together. By the fifth and sixth weeks, they were engaged in the course content, and I had one hundred percent attendance each and every day. But at the start of the seventh week, I was thrown a curveball.

I'd received a job offer from an application I'd made a year earlier, and for which I was previously rejected (Thanks Jason!). It was for a permanent full-time role as a sales trainer, for a telecommunications company, and was the job of my dreams (at the time).

I spoke to my group of students, and to the college and made my apologies, but I felt awful. A replacement trainer would be found, and the course would continue to run for the remaining six weeks.

I knew I was letting the group down by not finishing what we'd started, but at the same time, the new job was an opportunity I didn't want to pass up.

The next morning, one of the trainees approached me to ask a question on behalf of the group. She asked whether I would work with them to compress the final six weeks of content into three, so they could finish the course with me. She told me they'd all discussed it the previous night, and that if I agreed, they would put in an extra two hours per day (and do homework assignments) to get us through. It was an easy decision for me to make, and after three weeks of hard work, they all graduated.

At the time, and for some time afterwards, I believed she'd made the request because I was a good trainer (and they'd get an extra three weeks off) and whilst that may have been true, I now feel it had far more to do with us being connected as a team.

They'd forgotten the reason they were forced to be there and wanted to achieve the goals we'd set together during our first two weeks. They wanted to learn, and wanted to become proficient in retail, so they could go out and get jobs to change their lives.

On reflection, it was the most rewarding thing I've ever done, and I can now see that it was my leadership practices during those first two weeks which led to our success.

It's a formula I've used in every job I've had since, and a formula I still use today in my advisory, mentoring, and board roles.

The 'job of my dreams' as a sales trainer was both enjoyable and exhausting. I was charged with designing and delivering induction training for new contact centre staff, and every day for the following two years, I delivered a ten-day course to a new group of twelve trainees.

When I wasn't training, I was team leading, and when I wasn't team leading, I was making the training course better.

The role expanded into a national one, which in turn led to a series of other training and training management roles at various companies, which in turn led to a national training role with a financial services and technology company.

During the following years, I graduated from my psychology and education studies and branched out into organisational development and then into operations management, where I ended up leading a team of over three hundred frontline customer service staff.

That role took me to the UK to lead another team of three hundred, which in turn led to a global role leading thousands of people all over the world.

After three years overseas, I returned to Australia to head up Human Resources / People and Culture for about two thousand employees.

The single factor that has tied my career together has been my practice of supporting others to be what they wanted to be, and to achieve what they wanted to achieve. I've been afforded many opportunities and have achieved recognition with a number of awards; however, all of that pales into insignificance when I think about my experience with the group of unemployed trainees in regional Victoria.

For me, that was the essence of effective leadership.

My superpower is being able to see all the moving parts of a system, whilst noticing which parts effect other parts, especially as it relates to leadership.

I intuitively know which will succeed and which will fail, days, months, or years before they do. It's my blessing and it's my curse, and I'm still learning to let things play out to their end, regardless of their results, so that people can experience the system for themselves.

Experiential learning (learning through experience) is the most powerful type of learning as it's not happening in a book, in your ears, or on a screen; it's happening to you, and with you, firsthand.

I hope you may experience the nine leadership practices firsthand so you may know how they play out for you.

I wish you every success!

Quick Reference Guide

The nine principles of effective leadership

- i. Leadership is unlearning
- ii. Leadership is not management
- iii. Leadership is followership
- iv. Leadership must be individualised
- v. Leadership has no ego
- vi. Leadership ability doesn't come from technical ability
- vii. Leadership takes time
- viii. Leadership isn't a skill
- ix. Leadership is a practice

The nine practices for effective leadership

- i. Ask questions
- ii. Get to know your people
- iii. Empathy and compassion
- iv. Self-regulation
- v. Integrity
- vi. Tell the story
- vii. Engage
- viii. Steer
- ix. Boundaries

5Ds.com.au

published by inspirationism.com

www.ingramcontent.com/pod-product-compliance
Lightning Source LLC
Chambersburg PA
CBHW071251070526
44583CB00017B/2422